C000278502

AROUND
MARKET
HARBOROUGH
IN OLD PHOTOGRAPHS

DEDICATION

For Loreen and for Lynne:
friends, relations, guides and helpers.

AROUND
MARKET
HARBOROUGH
IN OLD PHOTOGRAPHS

COLLECTED BY
STEPH MASTORIS

Budding
BOOKS

A Budding Book

First published in 1989 by Alan Sutton Publishing Limited

This edition published in 1998 by Budding Books,
an imprint of Sutton Publishing Limited
Phoenix Mill · Thrupp · Stroud · Gloucestershire GL5 2BU

Copyright © Steph Mastoris, 1989

A catalogue record for this book is available from the British Library

ISBN 1-84015-049-1

Typesetting and origination by
Sutton Publishing Limited.
Printed in Great Britain by
WBC Limited, Bridgend, Mid-Glamorgan.

CONTENTS

INTRODUCTION

From the middle of the nineteenth century, amateur and professional photo-graphers have been recording places, people and events in and around Market Harborough. This book reprints a very small selection of the countless thousands of photographs which must have been taken locally between the 1850s and the 1960s. Most have been drawn from the extensive collection of original and copy prints held by the Harborough Museum, a branch of Leicestershire Museums, Arts and Records Service.

The photographs have been grouped around three general themes of everyday life, namely, places, people and events. They relate to both the town of Market Harborough and the ten or so villages within 5 miles of it, either side of the border between Leicestershire and Northamptonshire. The chronological bias is weighted towards the twentieth century. This has allowed photographs covering a wide range of subjects to be included, most never before published.

Material relating to each of the three themes has been sub-divided into a number of sections. The criteria for selecting the photographs has varied accordingly. The theme of 'places' starts off the book with two sections on topography and transport. The first concentrates on illustrating landmarks and buildings which no longer exist or have been radically changed. The second section on transport gives a general sketch of the various methods of commu-nication in the area before the widespread use of the motor car.

The core of the book is devoted to the theme of 'people' and has three sections which deal with education, earning a living and leisure. The first section looks at schools and their buildings around the town. In addition it attempts to show what children from a wide range of backgrounds actually looked like when attending school by reproducing class photographs from one decade – the 1920s. The section on earning a living demonstrates the wide range of occupations which have been carried on in Market Harborough over the last century and a half. It begins with manufacturing industry and progresses through the public services and private domestic service to agriculture, the market and retailing. The section on leisure covers sport, entertainment and 'culture', and again shows the large number of activities on offer in the area.

The concluding theme deals with 'events', both sad and happy. The first section concentrates on local activity during the First and Second World Wars. The surviving photographs suggest how formal were the events of the first conflict. There are the official photographs of the send-off and return of the troops, patriotic meetings and the dedication of war memorials. By contrast, the second war seems to be recorded only in snapshots, showing hasty glimpses of the 'home front' and the newcomers in the area; land girls, American servicemen and POWs. The book concludes on a happier note with a section on public celebrations and other communal events such as crowning village May queens and the Market Harborough Carnival.

Of course, none of these sections should be considered as dealing exclusively with one subject. Much of the fascination of historic photographs arises from spotting incidental details far removed from the main subject in the photographer's eye. Most of the photographs here contain considerable period information on costume, technology and local topography.

It is hoped that this collection of photographs will not be considered as purely an exercise in nostalgia. This book provides an opportunity for the Harborough Museum to share with a very wide public several hundred of the most interesting photographs in its collection. Furthermore, many prints are the only surviving record of aspects of the social history of the Harborough area. Indeed many pictures came to light during museum research projects where spoken testimony and photographic evidence were the only historical sources. Finally, these photographs allow us to contemplate the changes in daily life and the environment which have occurred since the 1850s. Although most changes are definitely for the better, some of these photographs show historically important and attractive buildings which have been destroyed for no real purpose. It is hoped that this book may help a little to foster greater concern for the careful development of our built environment now and in the future.

It is perhaps unnecessary to conclude that the Harborough Museum is always interested in receiving donations of historic photographs or borrowing such material for archival copying.

Streets, Villages and Landmarks

AERIAL VIEW OF MARKET HARBOROUGH, looking north, June 1935. The town dates from the middle of the twelfth century as a deliberately planned commercial centre where the road from Northampton to Leicester crossed the River Welland. Even in 1935 the size and plan of the town was little different from the medieval settlement. The spire of the medieval parish church still dominates the town centre, but now competes with the great mass of the nineteenth-century corset factory of R. & W.H. Symington. Long, thin 'burgage properties', laid out when the town was established, lie at right angles to the main market areas – the Square (south of the church) and the High Street (north of it). The main areas of growth are to the west ('New Harborough' of the 1870s), along St Mary's Road to the east and along the Northampton Road (in the parish of Little Bowden until 1900), to the south.

THE SQUARE, looking north, c. 1855. This is the earliest surviving photograph of Market Harborough. It was taken by a local pioneer photographer, the Revd William Law, rector of Marston Trussell (see p. 124). This print is one of three which Law took of the same scene, each slightly different. Note the oil-fired street lamp in the middle of the Square, which was one of several erected in the 1820s and called King Lamps. Gas lighting was introduced in 1833. The pump was only one of about three public pumps in the town. The posts and chains to the left were erected to keep animals from the western pavement on market days.

103.   High Street, Market Harborough.

THE HIGH STREET, looking north, c. 1953. The first five buildings on the left-hand side have now been demolished. Note the Brooke memorial on the extreme right of the picture at the junction with Church Square.

DISMANTLING THE BROOKE MEMORIAL FOUN-TAIN, c. 1955. This fountain was erected as a memorial to Sir William De Capell Brooke of Brooke House, in recognition of his philanthropy. It was first placed on the Square c. 1890 but was moved to Church Square in 1921 when the war memorial was erected. Removed again because of its nuisance to traffic (c. 1955), it was left in the Council yard for seven years until one of the Brooke family claimed it. It is now set up in Great Oakley Hall, the main residence of the Brookes.

THE SOUTH SIDE OF CHURCH SQUARE, 1933. The building in the centre of the picture (now occupied by the Harborough Theatre) was formerly the Green Dragon Inn. It included portions of a seventeenth-century structure, and there is a tradition that this was the priest's house in the Middle Ages.

THE EAST SIDE OF CHURCH SQUARE, c. 1914. The Dolphin Inn stands on the corner of Factory Lane and the west/east part of Adam & Eve Street (formerly called Tripe Alley). The inn is sandwiched between the two main buildings of the R. & W.H. Symington corsetry factory. It was demolished in 1936 when an extension to the right-hand factory (the 'Old Side') was built.

THE NORTH-EASTERN CORNER OF CHURCH SQUARE, 1933. These properties were demolished in December 1935 to create Roman Way. By the side of the shop with the awning is Burgess' Yard and the tunnel entrance led to Sun Yard.

SUN YARD, looking north, July 1935. This photograph was taken from the turret of the Symington factory, and shows the lay-out of Sun Yard. The central block of buildings were originally stables for the former Sun Inn the roof of which is at the bottom of the picture.

SUN YARD, looking south, 1933. The yard was developed by the late eighteenth century on land behind the Sun Inn. In 1881 32 households lived here.

ROMAN WAY in the course of construction, 1936. The whole of Sun Yard was demolished to create Roman Way. The remaining buildings on the left-hand side of the new road once formed the western side of Burgess' Yard.

THE EAST SIDE OF CHURCH STREET, August 1934. The long thin properties which run at right angles to the High Street and Church Street were established in the medieval period. Population pressure in the late eighteenth and nineteenth centuries caused their redevelopment as enclosed yards of small dwellings behind the larger buildings on the frontages.

THE REAR YARD OF KING'S HEAD PLACE, 1933. The lack of privacy and adequate sanitation, common to most of the yards of Harborough, is well illustrated in this photograph. Although the eight houses backing on to this yard were improved in 1934, they were not demolished until 1963.

RIDLEY'S YARD, looking east to the High Street, c. 1900. This yard, along with another on the left of the photograph (Coach and Horses' Yard) were demolished in 1902 to create Abbey Street.

ABBEY STREET, looking east to the High Street, c. 1904. This was the first major alteration in the town plan of Market Harborough in the modern period. The road was designed to link the High Street with the suburb of 'New Harborough' which was being built to the west of the Fairfield Road from the 1870s.

THE TOWN BROOK, c. 1925. A stream runs the length of the High Street, from the Folly Pond on the Leicester Road to the Welland. Until the mid-eighteenth century the stream was open and was used as a source of water for fire fighting. In the nineteenth century it was covered with a brick culvert and in 1925 this was replaced with a concrete pipe.

LEICESTER ROAD, looking north, c. 1920. A remarkably rustic scene, yet so close to the town. The Folly Pond lies behind the clump of trees on the left of the road in the middle distance.

THE MARKET HARBOROUGH UNION WORKHOUSE, Leicester Road, c. 1960. This workhouse was built in 1836 to provide accommodation for the poor of the 41 parishes which made up the Harborough Union. This portion of the building was demolished in 1975, but the rest of the site is used today as St Luke's Hospital.

THE SQUARE, looking south, April 1939. The roundabout was one of two created in 1937 as part of a reorganization of the Square.

DEMOLITION OF THE TANNERY CHIMNEY, 18 November 1965. A tannery was established on the north side of the Welland in the late 1860s, and for a century some sort of leather production or finishing took place here. This photograph was taken by Mr H. Webb, who was nearly killed when the chimney fell.

BRIDGE HOUSE, NORTHAMPTON ROAD, late 1960s. This substantial town house dates from before the 1830s. In later years it was used as a photographic studio and a lodging house for the female staff of Shindler's the drapers (on the Square). Although it was planned for demolition in 1946 to create a riverside walk, it was not pulled down until 1969.

MARKET HARBOROUGH RIVER WELLAND

WATER TOWER on the south side of the Welland, c. 1910 and, below, 1950s. This water tower was used to supply water to the greenhouses of Brooklands House, on Northampton Road, when it was the private residence of Samuel Symington, the proprietor of the soup and coffee factory.

FORMER COACH BUILDING WORKS, Northampton Road, early 1960s. The building stood to the south of the General Market and throughout the nineteenth century it was used as a carriage works and wheelwright's workshop. This façade of the building probably dates from the 1860s. It was demolished in the early 1970s.

HOUSES ON THE EAST SIDE of Northampton Road, 1954. The elegant Regency terrace of three-storey houses on the right have served as offices for the Symington's soup factory for most of this century. The three groups of dwellings on the left of the picture were demolished in the 1970s for additions to the Symington factory.

SPRINGFIELD STREET, looking west, c. 1910. The houses on the right were built in the 1880s for workers of the W. Symington soup and coffee factory. Beyond the terrace the imposing façade of the factory itself (built 1881) can be seen. The houses were demolished in the early 1960s.

RAILWAY BRIDGE at the north end of Northampton Road, 1938. Over this bridge ran the Rugby to Stamford branch of the LNWR, which was opened to Market Harborough in 1850. The flood water seen under the bridge was the result of one of the minor floods of the town on 9 August, when three-quarters of an inch of rain fell in 15 minutes and several shops were flooded. The bridge was demolished in 1970.

THE WELLAND PARK HOUSING ESTATE, 1934. The Welland Park estate was the second housing development created by the council to reduce slum conditions in the centre of the town. Between 1931 and 1934 100 houses were built along a new road which had been designed as a bypass for west to east through traffic. Further houses were erected by private builders.

CONTRASTING EDWARDIAN HOUSING: Northampton Road (above) and Lathkill Street (below), formerly Caxton Terrace, c. 1910. The 1890s saw the development of a sizeable suburb to the south of the town, along and to the west of the Northampton Road. It is interesting to compare the expensive detached and semi-detached villas built along the main road, with the more modest four- and five-room terraced houses erected in the newly laid out streets behind.

THE SQUARE, looking east, 1961. This row of shops dated from between the seventeenth and nineteenth centuries. All were demolished in 1962.

COVENTRY ROAD, looking towards the Square, 1935. The building painted white is the Bell Inn. The buildings beyond were built in the 1890s as part of a scheme to widen the road where it joined the Square.

COVENTRY ROAD, looking west, April 1915. The workmen are rebuilding the boundary wall of the 'Lilacs', which has been used as the Conservative Club since 1912.

COVENTRY ROAD BAPTIST CHAPEL, c. 1900. This chapel was erected in 1830 and replaced by the present art-nouveau building in 1907.

NORTH-EAST CORNER of the Square, June 1902. The street decorations are probably to celebrate the return of troops from the Boer War. Symington and Thwaites on the corner of Adam & Eve Street and St Mary's Road was the town's leading grocery shop.

REGENCY VILLA on the north side of St Mary's Road, 1958. This was one of several elegant town houses which were built along St Mary's Road, set well back from the thoroughfare. It was demolished in 1968 and the site is now used as the car park for the National Westminster Bank.

ST MARY'S ROAD, looking west (top) and east (bottom), 1914 and 1920s. The Oriental Cinema on the left-hand side of the eastern view was Market Harborough's second cinema and it opened in June 1921. In 1929 it was the first local cinema to show talking pictures. It closed in 1959.

BLAND'S STEAM FLOUR MILL, St Mary's Road, 1861. This steam flour mill was the first powered mill in the town, and was opened in 1857. Much of the building survives as part of the Harboro' Rubber works. The photograph looks south-west from the high ground by St Mary in Arden churchyard.

THE CHURCHYARD OF ST MARY IN ARDEN, 1959. Although St Mary's Church has been little used since the early seventeenth century, the cemetery was the only burial ground for Market Harborough until 1878. In 1956 it was decided to clear the area of headstones and this scheme was completed in the 1970s. Here members of the Market Harborough Historical Society are recording all the inscriptions on the headstones prior to their removal.

THE GREEN, GREAT BOWDEN, c. 1860. The photographer is standing south of the present church hall and looking north-west. On the left is Leicester Road and Sutton Road runs off to the right.

GUNNSBROOK POND, GREAT BOWDEN, c. 1910. This pond was situated on the south part of the Green and was used by both the ducks and the village blacksmith, whose house and workshop are in the background. The pond was filled in around 1928.

THE GREAT BOWDEN VILLAGE LOCK-UP, 1951. This lock-up was built in the 1800s and was situated at the side of cottages on the Langton Road. It was demolished in 1952. Standing next to the building is Frank Strongman, a leading light of the Market Harborough Historical Society and its honorary Curator (see p. 130).

THE GREEN, WESTON BY WELLAND, 1900s. Note the mud-walled cottage on the right of the picture. The cart belongs to F. Clements, Tripe and Ox Heel Dresser of Market Harborough.

DINGLEY HALL, c. 1910. The house was built on the site of a medieval preceptory of the Knights Hospitallers, and dates from the 1550s, with major additions in the 1680s. It is a fine example of the many large country houses in the Harborough area which attracted owners or tenants during the hunting season. Like many such houses it fell into disrepair after the Second World War but was refurbished in the 1970s.

BRAYBROOK, c. 1907. Looking north towards the village from the road to Arthingworth.

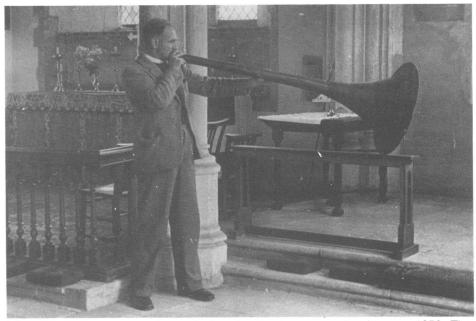

THE REVD RONALD LOXSTON demonstrating the Braybrook vamping horn, c. 1958. This curious instrument dates from the late seventeenth century. It was used to amplify the voices of the church choir and the leaders of metrical psalm singing. The horn is now on loan to the Harborough Museum.

AERIAL VIEW of the eastern fields of Little Bowden, looking north-west, 1945. The ridges and furrows of the pre-enclosure strip farming show up well. The Corby road (A427) runs across the upper portion of the picture while the Kettering road (A6) runs diagonally across the bottom left-hand corner. The railway can be seen in the top left-hand corner.

LITTLE BOWDEN CHURCH, mid-1860s. The church's wooden tower was replaced by the present stone bellcote in 1900. Note the workmen sharpening scythes in the churchyard.

THE RIVER JORDAN IN FLOOD, Little Bowden, July 1912. The photographer is looking south-east along the footpath connecting Scotland Road and Queen Street.

THE FORECOURT OF THE GEORGE HOTEL, Great Oxendon, 1930s. The cost of Cleveland petrol was 1s. 5½d. (7p) a gallon and the saloon car in the forecourt could be hired.

EAST FARNDON CHURCH, looking south, c. 1900. The mud-walled cottages in the foreground were demolished in 1935.

EAST FARNDON, looking south down the Harborough Road, July 1862. This early photograph gives some impression of the poor state of country roads in the nineteenth century. It also shows how widespread mud walls were in this area until the end of the century (note their protective thatch coping).

A PARTLY DEMOLISHED COTTAGE, East Farndon, 1951. The demolition of this brick cottage has revealed a timber 'cruck'; an earlier method of construction for the roof, using two semicircular beams joined at the apex.

LUBENHAM CHURCH, looking north-east, c. 1856. This photograph shows the eighteenth-century farmhouse to the north of the parish church before it was rebuilt in 1862 to create Tower House.

PAPILLON HALL, LUBENHAM, late 1940s. Known locally as 'Pamps' Hall, the house was originally built in the 1620s by a Huguenot fortifications engineer, David Papillon. The Hall was rebuilt by Sir Edwin Lutyens in 1902–4, but was demolished in 1951.

MAIN STREET, MARSTON TRUSSELL, looking west, 1875. Another photograph by the Revd William Law, who was rector here from 1842 to 1900 (see p. 124).

MARSTON TRUSSELL HALL, 1856.

MAIN STREET, LAUGHTON, 1942. The telephone pole on the right has a collection tin for waste bones to help in the war effort.

GUMLEY HALL, 1962. This was built in 1764 for Joseph Craddock, a friend of Dr Samuel Johnson and David Garrick, the actor. The collonade entrance porch dates from 1870. Like other large houses in the area it fell into disuse after the Second World War and was demolished in 1964.

AERIAL VIEW OF FOXTON, looking south-west, c. 1970. The Harborough arm of the Grand Union Canal runs east in an 'S' from Foxton Locks at the top of the photograph through the southern portion of the village.

THE BLACK HORSE INN, FOXTON, 1880s. This inn was rebuilt in 1900 to the design of H.W. Johnson, a local architect.

MAIN STREET, TUR LANGTON, looking south, c. 1910.

SECTION TWO

Transport

PASSING THROUGH FOXTON LOCKS, 1899. The flight of ten locks at Foxton was constructed between 1810 and 1814 with the intention of joining the Trent and Soar river navigations with the London to Birmingham canal system. In the top left-hand background can be seen the barge lift under construction.

THE LOWER ENTRANCE to Foxton Locks and the inclined plane barge lift, C. 1910. The barge lift was designed to reduce the time taken to travel the incline. This journey took about an hour using the locks, but only about 8 minutes on the barge lift.

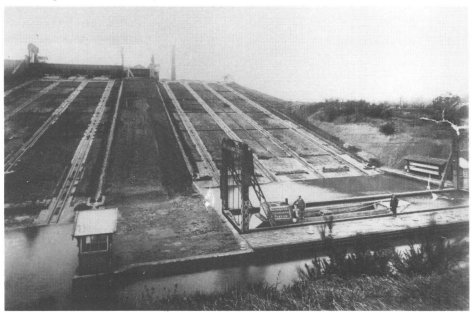

THE FOXTON INCLINED PLANE BARGE LIFT, 1900s. The lift was constructed between 1898 and 1900. It was a considerable feat of engineering, but not a commercial success. It ceased operation in 1910 and was dismantled in 1928.

THE COAL WHARVES at Foxton and Great Bowden, 1920s and, below, 1960. These two wharves served Foxton and Great Bowden. They were situated along the Harborough arm of the Grand Union Canal. This was constructed in 1809 as an extension of the canal from Leicester, before Foxton Locks took the route to London further south. The Foxton wharf continued to function until the 1940s.

THE MARKET HARBOROUGH CANAL BASIN, 1950. These photographs were taken during the first National Rally of canal boats, organized by the Inland Waterways Association in August 1950.

THE LEEDS TO LONDON EXPRESS near Great Bowden, August 1900. This double-headed passenger express is on the Midland Railway 'up' line to London. The first railway through Market Harborough was built in 1850 by the LNWR as part of its branch from Rugby to Stamford. In 1857 the Midland Railway opened its Leicester to London line (via Hitchin), which ran through the town. In 1859 the LNWR opened its line from Harborough to Northampton.

RAILWAY TUNNEL CONSTRUCTION at Great Oxendon, c. 1858. This horse-driven windlass is probably being used on the construction of the tunnel at Great Oxendon for the LNWR line from Market Harborough to Northampton. This route was opened in February 1859.

MARKET HARBOROUGH RAILWAY STATION, c. 1880. The station was rebuilt in its present form in 1884. The photographer is looking up the line to London and Rugby. The signals suggest that a London train is due.

MARKET HARBOROUGH JUNCTION, looking south-east, mid-1950s. A banking engine is assisting a coal train up an incline from Harborough to Oxendon and Kelmarsh on the Northampton line, possibly heading for Willesden, London. In the foreground are tube wagons from Stewarts & Lloyds in Corby and the points leading to the engine shed. In the background is the Harborough No. 2 signal box.

TRAIN SPOTTING AT MARKET HARBOROUGH STATION, mid-1950s. The train is the 'Thames–Clyde Express' heading for London.

AN EXCURSION down the Welland Valley in the 'Station Flies' leaves the Square, c. 1920. These 'flies' were owned by Arthur Wallis and used to transport people and goods to and from the railway station. Wallis is seated on the right-hand fly, the one following is driven by G.W. Tozer.

AN OMNIBUS EXCURSION leaves the High Street, c. 1920. Members of the Market Harborough Co-operative Society are departing on an excursion in buses provided by Kerr of Kettering and another company from Wellingborough. Regular motor bus services began in 1913 in the Harborough area and, by 1920, a considerable number of small companies were in business.

A BICYCLIST, c. 1905. Little is known about the owner of this curious machine with its odd pedalling system. The woman in the foreground is possibly the housekeeper to Sir Humphrey de Trafford of Hillcrest House on the Leicester Road.

AN AEROPLANE near Market Harborough, 25 June 1912. This is probably the second aeroplane to land near Market Harborough. It was piloted by Robert Slack who had to make a forced landing on the fields near the Wooden Bridge to the west of the Leicester Road.

SECTION THREE

Schooldays

MARKET HARBOROUGH GRAMMAR SCHOOL'S FIRST BUILDING, Church Square, 1920s. The school was established in 1607 by Robert Smyth, an Harborian who made his fortune in London in the 1580s. This purpose built school was erected in 1614 and was in use until 1909. The structure was extensively renovated in 1868 and refurbished in 1977.

MARKET HARBOROUGH GRAMMAR SCHOOL'S SECOND BUILDING, Coventry Road, 1960s. Overcrowding and lack of facilities led to the construction of this new building in 1892, by W.B. Bragg, a local chemist and school trustee. The building was used as a boarding house and general schoolroom while the old building in Church Square was used for chemistry and woodwork lessons. It was demolished in 1970.

Boys' Entrance. The County Grammar School, Market Harborough

MARKET HARBOROUGH GRAMMAR SCHOOL'S THIRD BUILDING, c. 1910. In 1909 a county council grammar school was established in Market Harborough and Smyth's school was amalgamated with this. For the first time local girls were able to receive a grammar school education.

Girls' Entrance. The County Grammar School, Market Harborough

STAFF AND PUPILS of the County Grammar School, 1924.

THE COOKERY ROOM at the County Grammar School, c. 1910. This photograph is from a series of postcards showing various classrooms in the school.

LITTLE BOWDEN SCHOOL, c. 1910. This was a combined infants and junior school built by the county council in 1907.

PUPILS OF LITTLE BOWDEN SCHOOL, 1927.

PUPILS OF MARKET HARBOROUGH ROMAN CATHOLIC SCHOOL, 1928. The Roman Catholic School was opened in Market Harborough in 1878.

A CLASSROOM AT FAIRFIELD ROAD SCHOOL, 1924. Fairfield Road School was established in 1838 by the non-conformist British and Foreign Schools Society. It was taken over by the county council in 1909.

STAFF AND PUPILS of a private school, c. 1920. In the centre sits Miss Janet Smith who ran this school at her house in Coventry Road. On the left of the group stands Kathleen Coales, a well known artist and book illustrator who worked as a teacher in the school.

THE MASTER OF GREAT BOWDEN SCHOOL, with his staff, c. 1880. Mr J. Smart was the schoolmaster from 1875 to 1886. His sister (seated) also taught in the school. On the far right is Clara Wilford, another assistant teacher.

GREAT BOWDEN SCHOOL, 1960s. This school was established in 1839 by the Anglican National Schools Society. The building was originally designed with accommodation for the Master in the centre, a classroom for boys on one side and girls on the other.

NATIONAL SCHOOL, Coventry Road, 1960s. This building was erected in 1836. The upper floor was added in 1842 as a separate classroom for girls. In 1894 the building was converted to use as an Oddfellows Hall. By the 1900s it was in use as the local Adult School.

SECTION FOUR

Earning a Living

THE FIRST SYMINGTON CORSET WORKSHOP in Plowman's Yard, 1935. This back-yard cottage was used by Sarah and James Symington to manufacture corsets from the mid-1830s until the 1860s.

THE FIRST SYMINGTON FACTORY in Factory Lane, 1962. A former worsted and carpet factory in 1805 was partly occupied by Robert and William Henry Symington (sons of Sarah and James) in 1865 to carry on the family corset business. By 1877 the firm occupied all the building and, in 1881, an extra three storeys were added. The northern (left-hand) portion of the factory was added in 1936. The whole building was demolished in 1973.

R. & W.H. SYMINGTON: marking out corsetry cloth ready for cutting, c. 1930. Here Tom Goode draws around pattern templates to mark cutting lines on 'lays' of cloth, often 20 to 30 thicknesses deep. Mr Goode started work in 1913 in Symington's at the age of 14. After two years sweeping up cuttings and two years finding patterns for others, he undertook a three-year apprenticeship as a marker out. Apart from war service, he continued in this job from 1920 until 1975.

R. & W.H. SYMINGTON: the printing room, 1920s. This room was situated in a part of the factory on the north of Adam and Eve Street and is now occupied by the Harborough Museum.

R. & W.H. SYMINGTON: the cutting room, c. 1900. Here the marked out 'lays' of cloth are being cut up. The cutters use long, razor sharp knives. By the 1920s these were replaced by motor driven band knives. As with marking out and printing, cutting was a job done solely by men.

R. & W.H. SYMINGTON: sewing, c. 1908. Here the cut pieces of fabric are being sewn together to form the garment. The firm was one of the first in Britain to use sewing machines for manufacturing corsetry.

R. & W.H. SYMINGTON: ironing corsets, c. 1914. Here the finished corsets are being ironed. By the 1920s this job had become mechanized.

R. & W.H. SYMINGTON: shaping c. 1908. Here the completed corsets are being starched and shaped on heated copper forms known as 'Swedish maidens'.

WILLIAM SYMINGTON'S COFFEE MILL, Springfield Street, c. 1870. William Symington set up business in Market Harborough as a tea dealer and grocer in 1827. By 1850 he had established a factory on the Northampton Road for roasting coffee and making pea flour. He supplied the British Army with pea flour during the Crimean War and this continued prosperity led to the enlargement of the factory in 1881. By 1919 no more coffee was roasted here and production centred on dried soup, gravy and table jellies and creams.

SAMUEL SYMINGTON, c. 1900. He was the son of William Symington and head of the firm from his father's death in 1898 until his own demise in 1909.

W. SYMINGTON: soup packing, 1930s. These women are filling soup packets by hand. Note the scales and funnel at each packing table. Mechanized packing only began in the 1940s. There was a 6d. (2½p) reward for finding a weevil in the soup powders.

W. SYMINGTON: a staff presentation, C. 1946. Miss Rowan (centre) was supervisor of the Girls' Department (mainly packing) for 18 years. To the left is Kenneth Symington and to the right is Beatrice Timson, a representative of the Girls' Department.

W. SYMINGTON: export packing, late 1960s. Here Jack Coleman is packing boxes of gravy improver for export to Canada.

W. SYMINGTON: an aerial view of the factory, looking east, 1948. Northampton Road runs across the foreground and Springfield Street is on the extreme right. The original factory was close to the chimney and the extension of 1881 faces Springfield Street. The buildings to the left of the chimney were built between 1927 and 1932 and included a packing room, canning room and canteen.

HARBORO' RUBBER: the storage area behind the Works, 1929. The Harboro' Rubber Company was established in 1894 by Arthur Briggs as a subsidiary to the family boot and shoe firm in Leicester. Until the 1930s the firm concentrated on making rubber soles, heels, bicycle pedals and solid tyres. The works were known as the Day and Night Mills because of its 24-hour shift system, and this gave rise to the firm's 'Dainite' trade name.

HARBORO' RUBBER: the front of the Works, St Mary's Road, 1929. The factory was begun in Bland's steam flour mill (see p. 32) in the centre of the photograph. The extension on the left was erected in 1925.

HARBORO' RUBBER: the mill room, 1929. Here raw rubber is being mixed with vulcanizing chemicals and rolled into sheets for pressing.

HARBORO' RUBBER: the press room, 1929. Here shoe soles are being cut from the sheets of rubber compound. The heated press used also vulcanizes the material.

HARBORO' RUBBER: the trimming room, 1929. Here the 'flash' is being trimmed from the shoe soles and heels and they are checked for defects.

HARBORO' RUBBER: stores and packing room, 1908.

HARBORO' RUBBER: a consignment of solid rubber tyres, c. 1920. The firm began manufacturing solid rubber tyres during the First World War and continued to do so until the late 1920s.

TUNGSTONE: aerial view of the factory, looking north, 1960s. Lathkill Street is on the top right and Bath Street (almost hidden) forms the northern boundary of the Tungstone Works. The factory began in 1898 as a foundry for printing type, the first in Britain to use the American point system of sizing. By 1917 the firm was making a wide range of precision die cast metal and wood products, including lead accumulator batteries. These became the major concern of the company, which changed its name to Tungstone in 1925.

TUNGSTONE: exterior of the main building, 1930s.

TUNGSTONE: battery assembly, c. 1960. Here battery grids are being prepared for covering with a lead oxide paste.

TUNGSTONE: battery assembly, c. 1960. Here battery grids are being prepared for covering with a lead oxide paste.

TUNGSTONE: publicity delivery van, c. 1960.

THE TANNERY, 1880s. The tannery was situated near the south-west corner of the Square, close to the north bank of the River Welland, ensuring a constant water supply. No tanning took place on the site after 1913, although leather finishing was carried on here until the 1960s. Here oak bark is about to be pulverized for use in the tanning vats.

PART OF THE TANNERY after a fire, 1905.

HOPTON'S BENT TIMBER WORKS, c. 1928. In 1907 this business moved from the canal basin to a site on Gores Lane. The firm specialized in the curing and steaming of timber. Here coffin boards are being dried (above), while the bending gang (below) can be seen wearing sack aprons to protect their clothes from the wet timber.

WILLEY'S WOOL WAREHOUSE, St Mary's Road, 1920s. Large bales of fleeces are being transported from the warehouse.

A HOSIERY FACTORY in Highfield Street, late 1920s. This factory is one of several light industrial concerns which developed in the town from the late nineteenth century. Others included Crosby Valves and Loomes' boots and shoes.

ELLIS & EVERARD'S WAREHOUSE AND YARD, St Mary's Road, c. 1920. In the 1970s this firm moved its premises across the road to Clarence Street, on the site of the former gas works.

EADY & DULLEY'S BREWERY, Northampton Road, c. 1900. The brewery was established in the early nineteenth century and occupied a large site on the south side of the river. It was closed down in the early 1900s and the buildings demolished in 1908. The site remained unused until 1960 when it was used for the bus station.

AN EADY & DULLEY STEAM DRAY, C. 1900.

AN ESTATE CARPENTER at Marston Trussel, 1861. One of a series of portraits of manual workers in Marston Trussell made by the Revd William Law. The subject is probably William Adnitt, jr., a master carpenter living in the village.

DEMOLISHING A MUD-WALL HOUSE at Laughton, c. 1947. The left-hand workman is 'Patsy' Garton, a local builder and carrier.

DEMOLISHING EADY & DULLEY'S BREWERY, Northampton Road, 1908.

A CHIMNEY SWEEP and his family, Adam and Eve Street, 1923. Mr W.F. Swinton and his family are standing outside their house. Adam and Eve Street and the adjoining Quakers Yard was a centre for the town's chimney sweeps throughout the late nineteenth century. The Swinton's home was demolished in 1932.

MARKET HARBOROUGH TOWN REFUSE COLLECTORS, 1927. This is one of two horse-drawn collection vehicles which were purchased by the council in 1927 as part of its major attack on the town's refuse problem. In the same year a destructor was opened at St Mary's Bridge and the use of regulation ash bins made compulsory for all householders.

THE PUBLIC BATHS being pumped with river water, 1944. The public baths on Northampton Road were erected in 1896. During the Second World War they were used to store river water for emergency fire fighting. Here the long-serving Baths Superintendant, Jack Foster, is filling the baths with the Fire Brigade's steam pump of 1905.

MARKET HARBOROUGH FIRE BRIGADE, 1904. The town has been served by a formal volunteer fire brigade since at least the 1870s. Here the force is seen standing proudly outside their new fire station in Abbey Street.

THE MARKET HARBOROUGH DIVISION of the Leicestershire Constabulary, 1933. In the centre is Superintendent J.W. Mee.

THE MARSTON TRUSSELL POSTMAN, 1861. Another portrait by the Revd William Law showing mid-nineteenth-century occupational costume.

FOUR SERVANTS at Marston Trussell Hall, C. 1910. An interesting example of different clothes for different occupations. These servants are (from left to right): the gardener, the butler, the footman and the game keeper.

INDOOR SERVANTS at Noseley Hall, mid-1930s. The staff are carrying out an August 'spring clean' of the whole house while the family is away in Scotland. They are (left to right): the school-room maid, third housemaid, footman, head housemaid and second housemaid. Standing on the bay window are the odd man and the estate carpenter.

A COWMAN ON THE MARSTON TRUSSELL ESTATE, 1861. Note the smock frock worn by many agricultural labourers until the end of the nineteenth century.

THE SIGN POST AT LAUGHTON GREEN, 1954. Throughout the nineteenth and early twentieth centuries the agriculture of the upper Welland Valley around Market Harborough was dominated by the fattening of beef cattle and sheep. Note how every road out of Laughton is gated, showing the extent of surrounding pasture.

MARKET HARBOROUGH AND DISTRICT FARMERS on an outing to Port Sunlight, 1934. Some of the leading graziers of the Harborough Area are in this group.

SELLING CATTLE IN THE HIGH STREET, C. 1900. The Harborough market was essential to the graziers' work. Unfattened 'store' cattle would be bought in the early spring and fattened on the lush Welland Valley pastures. The beasts would then be sold for meat in the autumn and early winter.

SELLING HIGHLAND CATTLE at Market Harborough cattle market, C. 1910. This posed photograph records the conclusion of a sale. The buyer and seller are about to slap hands on the deal. In fact, very few Highland cattle were ever sold in the Harborough Market.

A HERD OF PEDIGREE SHORTHORN DAIRY CATTLE at Hall Farm, Shangton, c. 1952. Shorthorns were a popular breed in the Harborough area until the late 1960s.

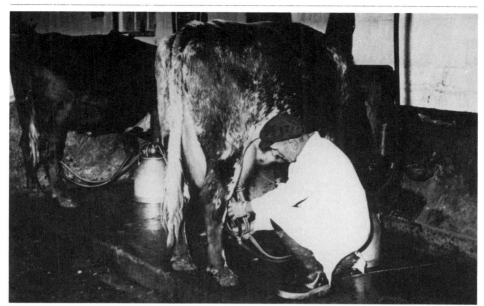

MILKING SHORTHORN CATTLE at Hall Farm, Shangton, c. 1952. The herdsman, Ernest Hall, is using individual bucket milking machines.

SHEARING SHEEP AT SMEETON WESTERBY, c. 1930. The hand-driven shearing machine is being turned by Joe Higgs while Bruce Hill removes the fleece.

HARVESTING CORN AT SHANGTON, 1920s. A horse-drawn reaper binder cuts the corn and binds it into small sheaves.

CARTING AWAY THE HAY HARVEST, SHANGTON, 1920s. Horses were the main source of motive power on local farms until the late 1940s.

PRISONERS OF WAR LOADING HAY at Kelmarsh, 1943. Here small heaps ('cobs') of hay are being carted away. Note the 'PW' on the shirt of the left-hand prisoner.

THE LIVESTOCK MARKET on the Square, *c.* 1900. The weekly livestock market was held here and in the High Street until 1903. Before the 1880s this area was called the Sheep Market.

MOVING CATTLE ON THE SQUARE, 1900. The weekly livestock sales in the centre of the town resulted in increasing disruption to daily commercial life and posed a considerable public health problem.

THE CATTLE MARKET, 1903. In 1903 the District Council opened its purpose-built cattle market on land between the river and Springfield Street.

MARKET STALLS ON THE SQUARE, c. 1930. After the departure of the livestock market from the Square, the space was used by the covered stalls erected on Tuesdays and Saturdays. Formerly these had been sited at the bottom of High Street and in Church Square.

THE GENERAL MARKET BUILDING under construction, 1938. In 1938 a covered market was erected on part of the cattle market site, facing the Northampton Road. Henceforth no stalls could be erected on the Square.

EMERY'S MILLINERY SHOP, north-east side of the Square, c. 1865. From at least the eighteenth century, Market Harborough has been a centre for retailing as well as general marketing, and the small independent shopkeeper has played a very important part in the development and administration of the town.

T.B. HUNT'S FISH SHOP, Church Square, early 1920s. T.B. Hunt ran a large fishmongering business, based in Leicester, with branches in Market Harborough, Wigston and Melton Mowbray. In 1920 the Harborough branch was sold to MacFisheries.

THE PURE DAIRY SUPPLY COMPANY, High Street, c. 1910. This shop was on the west side of the High Street, next to the entry leading into Dairy Yard. The shop's dairy was situated on the north of this yard. The business ran a milk round throughout the town.

SYMINGTON AND THWAITES' GROCERY SHOP on the corner of Adam and Eve Street and St Mary's Road, c. 1932. The firm was started by Walter Symington, nephew of James and William Symington, and George Thwaites in 1878. This splendid corner premises was opened in 1894, and continued in business as a high class grocer until 1960.

SYMINGTON AND THWAITE'S BRANCH SHOP, the Green, Great Bowden, c. 1938. This was the only branch shop opened by the firm. It closed in 1948.

MARKET HARBOROUGH CO-OPERATIVE SOCIETY main shop, the High Street, c. 1920. The Market Harborough Co-operative Society was established in 1862 and opened its first shop on Church Square, selling groceries and provisions. In 1892 it opened this large shop on the High Street and, for 75 years, it was the town's only general department store. The building was rebuilt in the mid-1970s.

THE PROVISIONS COUNTER, Market Harborough Co-op main shop, c. 1910.

THE FIRST BRANCH SHOP of the Market Harborough Co-operative Society, 1908. The Co-op opened its first branch shop in Great Bowden in the late 1890s. In 1908 the premises were moved to a purpose-built shop on the Green, next to the Shoulder of Mutton pub. By 1914 the Society had four other branches outside the town.

THE STAR SUPPLY STORES, the Square, c. 1910. The Star was the first of the major national grocery shops to open in Market Harborough.

J. STOKES' SHOP on the corner of St Mary's Road and the lane leading to Dingley Terrace, c. 1910. This is typical of the many local corner shops which opened as Market Harborough's suburbs developed in the 1880s. Note the hand cart for deliveries – an important part of customer service.

W. FALKNER & SON'S SHOP, High Street, c. 1910. The Falkner family had been making and selling boots and shoes in Market Harborough from at least the 1830s. In 1901 they moved into these premises, where they remained until the business closed in 1987. The interior of the workroom behind the shop has been recreated in the Harborough Museum.

A TRADE STAND OF CLARK & SON, SADDLERS, C. 1900. From the 1840s, three generations of Clarks worked as saddlers in the town. The Pugh family, who started off as their apprentices, subsequently took over the business.

R.J. WEBB & CO'S SHOP AND FACTORY, the Square, 1960s. The Webb brothers ran the main photographic processing business in the area. The firm also undertook studio work, electrical installation and published postcards and books. The business started in the back room of a house in Caxton Street in 1920. The firm moved to the Square in 1928 and continued there until it closed in 1972.

JOHN JESSON'S BUTCHERY SHOP, Gumley, 1905. Jesson was a grazier who ran a small butchery business between 1894 and 1910. To the left of his house is the purpose-built shop with a slaughter house behind. The trap was used for deliveries to the nearby villages of Foxton, Laughton and Mowsley. Jesson's is a fine example of the village butchers' businesses which were widespread until the 1930s.

GEORGE GARDINER'S DELIVERY VAN, c. 1910. Gardiner ran a general grocery, bakery and carting business at Nelson Street from the late 1870s. His shop also acted as a sub-post office for the western suburb of 'New Harborough'.

GEORGE BARWELL and his carrier's van on the road to Uppingham, c. 1910. Until the 1920s horse-drawn carriers' carts were an essential way of transporting goods to and from farms, villages and towns.

'DOING THE ROUNDS', Foxton, c. 1900. The cart of a carrier or delivery man stands outside a cottage and orders for goods are being taken.

AN ICE-CREAM VENDOR on the Square, mid-1920s. Antonio Di Fazio set up his ice-cream business in Adam and Eve Street in 1909. Until he retired in 1927, he was a familiar figure selling ices around the streets of Market Harborough.

TINKER KNIFE GRINDERS near Great Bowden, 1920s. This rare photograph of tinkers was taken by the local artist Kathleen Coales.

SECTION FIVE

Leisure

THE BOXER JACK GARDNER at a celebration dinner, 7 December 1950. This dinner was held to celebrate Jack Gardner's winning of the British and Empire Heavyweight Boxing Championship. He was born in Market Harborough in 1936 and died in 1972.

R. & W.H. SYMINGTON & CO'S SPORTS GROUND, 1952. This ground was opened in 1921 and has been a valuable recreational facility for the whole town ever since. The original facilities included football, hockey and cricket pitches, a bowling-green, tennis-courts and a bandstand.

THE TEAM OF HARBOROUGH ATHLETIC FOOTBALL CLUB, 1920s. This was a junior club which was active in the 1920s.

A MEET OF THE FERNIE HUNT AT GUMLEY HALL, c. 1910. Until the middle of the nineteenth century, the Harborough area was hunted by the Quorn. However in the 1850s a break-away group established itself here and, by the 1920s, it was known as the Fernie.

THE KENNELS OF THE FERNIE HUNT, Great Bowden, late 1920s. These were purpose-built by the Hunt in 1924.

A BOATING PARTY on the Harborough canal, c. 1910. The River Welland is far too small and shallow to allow any form of boating. However, the Harborough extension of the Grand Union Canal has been used for pleasure boating since the late nineteenth century.

THE MARKET HARBOROUGH REGATTA, 1909. The first regatta was held on the canal in 1905 and similar events took place annually for the next decade or so.

BOY SCOUTS FROM THE MARKET HARBOROUGH TROOP at camp, c. 1913. The first troop of Market Harborough boy scouts was established in 1908.

WOMEN BICYCLISTS, c. 1900. This photograph probably shows members of the Market Harborough Bicycle Club on an excursion. The club was established sometime around 1890.

LITTLE BOWDEN RECREATION GROUND, 1930s. This recreation ground was created by the council in 1905. The bandstand was demolished in the early 1950s.

MARKET HARBOROUGH TOWN BAND, 1890s. The first civilian town band was formed in 1897. However, this photograph might show the Little Bowden band which was founded in 1888.

DEMOLITION OF THE FORMER PHILANTHROPIC HALL, the Square, c. 1970. The Philanthropic Hall was built in 1872 by the local Temperance Society to accommodate a coffee house and reading room. In the 1890s it was used by the local Liberal Party for major meetings but, in 1906, it was partly converted into a roller skating rink. The whole building was converted into the County Electric Cinema in 1911.

THE PALESTINE EXHIBITION at the Assembly Rooms, May 1910.

JOHN BLAND AS THE 'PIRATE KING', 1899. Bland (later the author of *Byegone Days in Market Harborough*) was one of the regular performers with the Market Harborough Operatic Society. This was formed in 1898 and gave annual performances of Gilbert and Sullivan operas until 1911. The society was revived in 1948.

THE SYMINGTON ORCHESTRA, 1948. This small group of amateur musicians was formed from the workforce of the R. & W.H. Symington corset factory. It was yet another example of the wide range of social and leisure activities fostered by this very paternalistic company.

AN AMATEUR PHOTOGRAPHER AT WORK, High Street, c. 1915. Here Viscountess Downe of Dingley Hall is taking a photograph of the War Workers' Depôt in the High Street. The depôt was the centre for women's voluntary work in Harborough during the First World War.

THE REVEREND WILLIAM LAW and Eliza his wife, 1870s. Law was rector of Marston Trussell parish from 1842 to 1900, but he was also a keen and accomplished pioneer amateur photographer. His work dates from the mid-1840s to the 1890s, with a break in the 1880s. He experimented with several techniques including daguerreotypes, calotypes and the wet collodian process.

MRS ELIZA LAW AND HER CHILDREN, c. 1860. The Laws had seven children in all. The oldest two, William and Mary, stand either side of their mother.

ERNEST ELLIOTT PERFORMING HIS HUMAN MARIONETTE ACT, 1930s. Although a tailor by trade, Ernest Elliott was an extremely talented musician and performer of comic songs. His Human Marionettes were an ingenious combination of his own head and a stick puppet. He performed regularly from 1922 to 1957 and his acts are still warmly remembered.

CROWDS OUTSIDE THE COUNTY ELECTRIC CINEMA, the Square, 1921. The County Electric Cinema was the first permanent cinema in Market Harborough. It was housed in the old Philanthropic Hall on the Square and opened in November 1911. Note the base of the war memorial under construction behind the hoarding on the left of the crowd.

THE FAÇADE OF THE FORMER PHILANTHROPIC HALL and County Electric Cinema, early 1960s. The 'County' closed in 1939, soon after the opening of the Ritz on Northampton Road. The building ended its life as an antiques shop and was demolished in the early 1970s.

THE VICTORIAN PARLOUR DISPLAY at the Coronation Exhibition in the Market Harborough Museum, June 1953. The Market Harborough Historical Society was set up in 1931 and, from 1938 until 1974, it maintained a museum in an upper room of the town library on the Square. This collection was transferred to the Harborough Museum when it was established by Leicestershire Museums Service in 1983.

JOHN FOTHERGILL presenting the manuscripts of his memoirs to the museum, c. 1950. Fothergill (left), an eccentric hotelier and author, came to the town in 1934 and, until 1953, was owner/manager of the Three Swans. Next to him are Frank Strongman, the curator, and Mr Reeds, the Secretary of the Historical Society.

MEMBERS OF THE HISTORICAL SOCIETY discussing fieldwork, *c*. 1950. Over the years members of the Society have carried out a number of excavations and fieldwork projects. Here the President of the Society, Canon Redlich (left), Mr Reeds (middle) and Frank Strongman (right) discuss fieldwork with Kathleen Kenyon.

MEMBERS OF THE HISTORICAL SOCIETY on an excursion, *c*. 1960.

FRANK STRONGMAN AND THE MOWSLEY STONE, c. 1953. Strongman was a founder member of the Historical Society and was its honorary curator until his death in 1956. Here he contemplates the Mowsley Stone, one of a number of local landmarks which featured in his research into prehistoric 'astronomy'. Besides being on a local ley line, the stone was supposed to turn over when Theddingworth Church clock struck thirteen.

The Two World Wars

THE 'HARBOROUGH BOYS' GO TO WAR, 6 August, 1914. 'E' Company of the 5th Leicestershire Regiment, (Harborough Territorials) parade on the Square, prior to marching to Loughborough to meet with other companies from Leicestershire. Two days after the outbreak of war this was the first detachment of Market Harborough men to go to war.

A GROUP OF NEW RECRUITS at the rear of the Territorial HQ on the Coventry Road, 1915. Left to right, back row: Ernie Coleman, Sam Fellows. Middle row: Smith, George Chapman, -?-, Wood, Eric Carter, Jack Gregory. Front row: Sid Bale, P. Horsley, Ernie 'Josie' Wilson, -?-, Albert Green.

PAY DAY FOR THE HARBOROUGH TERRITORIALS, 1914. This photograph was taken on Belmont Road, Luton, where the Territorials were billeted. Captain Harold Jeffries is seated at the table, with him is Sgt. Jacques. Colour Sgt. Jelley calls out the names.

KIT INSPECTION AT THE LUTON BILLET, 1914. A group of Harborough Territorials at Luton, left to right: Fred Tuffs, Bill Bailey, Mark Teasdale, 'Bob' Cotton.

TWO HARBOROUGH TERRITORIALS at the Front in France, 1915. Ernest Downes (sitting) died when a revolver, being cleaned by another soldier, went off. His companion is Fred Allen.

WRITING HOME FROM EGYPT, 1916. Sergeant Ernest Capell, RAMC, was a prominent member of the local St John's Ambulance. He enlisted at the beginning of the war and not only served in Egypt but also in the Dardanelles. His wife and son are shown in the top right.

THE ASSEMBLY ROOM, after a patriotic meeting. At least two such meetings were held (in 1914 and 1915) to urge men to enlist. The first was well attended, the second was not.

SHOOTING PRACTICE FOR THE VOLUNTEERS, c. 1915. A group of Market Harborough Volunteers at a rifle range in Little Bowden brickyard. The Volunteers were formed in December 1914 and were similar to the Home Guard of the Second World War, including men too old, too young or otherwise exempt from military service.

BELGIAN REFUGEES WITH FATHER KAVANAGH, 1914. In the autumn of 1914 Market Harborough took in a group of refugees from Belgium and they were given a house in Abbey Street, where they stayed throughout the war. Father Kavanagh was the priest in charge of the local Roman Catholic Church.

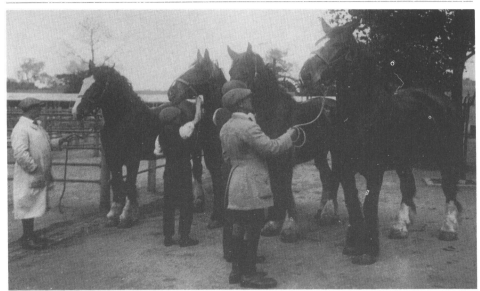

THE REMOUNT DEPÔT at the cattle market, 1915. Within days of the outbreak of war, the cattle market was turned into the Remount Depôt for the supply of horses to the army. Initially, the horses were stabled in marquees but, later, wooden buildings were erected. Captain Clarke was officer in charge. In 1917 some Mexicans served here and gave displays of their riding skills at local gymkhanas.

A MOTOR AMBULANCE funded by Market Harborough & District farmers, c. 1915. This vehicle was probably provided by local farmers as part of the national fund-raising effort by the British Farmers Red Cross Fund.

DEDICATION OF THE MARKET HARBOROUGH WAR MEMORIAL, Sunday 25 September 1921. The memorial was designed by W. Talbot Brown of Wellingborough and was paid for by public subscription. Originally the architect designed the memorial without plaques for the names of the dead. This provoked a lively correspondence in the local newspapers and the plaques were finally added. The residue of the money collected also paid for the memorial wing of the cottage hospital. In the crowd on the left is a cameraman from the cinematic firm of Cardeaux (Coventry) who made a newsreel film of the event which still survives.

CIVIC WELCOME FOR RETURNING SERVICEMEN, August 1919. The first event of a two-day celebration for the returning servicemen. Eight hundred were given dinner at the Assembly Rooms but, due to shortage of space, tables had to be erected outside in Abbey Street.

AFTER THE DEDICATION OF THE WAR MEMORIAL, 25 September 1921. Seen here are wreaths from families and friends of the 248 Harborians who were killed during the war.

EVACUEES ARRIVING AT MARKET HARBOROUGH STATION, September 1939. Over 3,000 mothers, children and teachers were evacuated to the Harborough area during the month following the outbreak of war. However, when the expected aerial bombardment of the cities did not occur immediately, many returned home.

THE MARKET HARBOROUGH HOME GUARD, c. 1941. The Harborough battalion of the Leicestershire Home Guard was established in the summer of 1940. This photograph was taken outside its HQ, the Drill Hall on Coventry Road (formerly the second grammar school building).

SEWING PARACHUTES AT R. & W.H. SYMINGTON, 1940s. During the Second World War the company produced over one million troop and supply parachutes.

LAND GIRLS THRESHING THE HARVEST AT LUBENHAM, 1940s. The Women's Land Army made important contributions to the war effort. Many lived on individual farms, but there was an area hostel for the rest at Lubenham.

WORKS POSTER at R. & W.H. Symington for the National Savings campaign, 1941.

GAS DECONTAMINATION SQUAD of Harborough Urban District Council, 1943. Here the squad are involved in an exercise on decontaminating food at the treatment depôt in the Cattle Market.

AIR RAID STRETCHER PARTY, 1943. Extensive air raid precautions had been made from the first threat of war in 1938. Thankfully, no bombardment of the town occurred.

A COMPLAINT ABOUT FOOD CONTROLS in Emerson's cafe, early 1940s. The sign amid the buns in the window reads, 'This is Tuesday's waste. M[inistry] O[f] F[ood] refuse to allow it to be sold off units. When unfit to be sold as food it can then be destroyed.'

A GROUP OF GERMAN PRISONERS OF WAR, c. 1946. German prisoners of war arrived in the Harborough area in 1945; the main camp was on the outskirts of the town on the Farndon Road. Other camps were located at Naseby, Harrington, Brixworth and Stoughton.

THE EAST FARNDON POW CAMP FOOTBALL TEAM, c. 1946. This team played those in other camps. Although it was illegal for prisoners to play with the locals, several villages benefitted from talented German players secreted in their teams.

A GERMAN POW at work on a Lubenham farm. This ex-Luftwaffe pilot is driving reputedly the first combine harvester in Leicestershire. He came to Harborough in 1946 as a POW and elected to stay on as a Free Worker in 1948. He eventually married an evacuee and settled in the town.

ITALIAN PRISONERS OF WAR, C. 1944. Italian POWs first came to the Harborough area in 1942 or 1943. Until 1946 their main local camp was on the Farndon Road, which was later used for German POWs.

YANKS AND RAF DRINKING IN LUBENHAM, C. 1944. Sections of the 82nd Airborne Division of the US Army were based in the Harborough area during the build up to D-Day. These formed the main contingent of American troops which came to the Harborough area during the war.

LAND GIRLS AND RAF PERSONNEL on the runway of Husbands Bosworth airfield, C. 1943. This airfield was a satellite of the Market Harborough station at Foxton (Gartree).

NO. 63 HOME AMBULANCE TRAIN at Great Bowden siding, March 1941. This train was virtually a complete military hospital on wheels. The first four coaches formed living accommodation for 24 personnel and the remaining seven coaches acted as wards. The train was stationed at Great Bowden from July 1940 to October 1941.

'VICTORY IN EUROPE' PARADE through the Square, 13 May 1945. Seen here are detachments of the Women's Land Army and the Market Harborough Home Guard. The salute was taken from the traffic roundabout on the right.

SECTION SEVEN
Celebrations

PRESENTING SOUVENIRS OF THE CORONATION OF GEORGE V, June 1911. Throughout the history of the town, the Square has been used for public celebrations and other mass gatherings.

MAY DAY AT MARSTON TRUSSEL, 1910 (above) and 1890 (below). The Revd William Law stands behind the May Queen in the bottom photograph.

CROWNING THE MAY QUEEN OF MARSTON TRUSSELL, 1900 and 1954.

REHANGING THE BELLS OF GREAT BOWDEN CHURCH, 1925.

REPLACING THE WEATHERCOCK of Market Harborough Parish Church, 1911. In the centre of this group is Miss Akiens who climbed the spire to replace the weathercock.

CELEBRATION DINNERS for male and female staff of R. & W.H. Symington, 1950s. The men are members of the company's fishing club but the reason for the women's staff gathering is not known.

A HOLY DAY at the Roman Catholic School, Market Harborough, c. 1901.

A STREET PARTY FOR THE CORONATION OF ELIZABETH II, Caxton Street, June 1953.

A FRIENDLY SOCIETY PARADE outside the Coach and Horses pub, Lubenham, c. 1883. Here the members of Triumph Lodge No. 179 of the Oddfellows assemble for their annual Whitsun church parade. All the Lodge's meetings were held in the Coach and Horses, formerly the Swan Inn.

THE FIRST QUEEN OF THE MARKET HARBOROUGH CARNIVAL, 1931. The Harborough Carnival was established in the early 1930s to raise funds for the Cottage Hospital on the Coventry Road. Each queen (Dorothy Gilbert here) was chosen from contestants picked at carnival dances held in villages throughout the area.

A FLOAT FROM THE HARBOROUGH CARNIVAL, C. 1931. This float highlights one of the problems of the Market Harborough Cottage Hospital.

FLOATS FROM THE HARBOROUGH CARNIVAL by Tungstone and the Market Harborough Co-operative Society, 1931 and 1948. The carnival provided an opportunity for local businesses to indulge in friendly rivalry by producing the most imaginative float each year.

ENTRANTS IN THE HARBOROUGH CARNIVAL, late 1930s. The two giants are possibly the creation of the local police force. Gardiner's was a leading firm of home furnishers with a shop on the north side of St Mary's Road.

ACKNOWLEDGEMENTS

This book would not have been possible without the generosity of many people who donated these photographs to the Harborough Museum, or loaned them for copying. Their names are listed below and apologies are offered in advance for any inadvertent omissions.

Great credit must also go to the honorary curators of the Market Harborough Historical Society who collected and preserved many of the early photographs reproduced here. They were Frank Strongman (1938–56), A.G. Coltman (1956–77) and Geoffrey Brandwood (1978–82).

Many of the remaining photographs were acquired by Sam Mullins, the first professional curator of the Harborough Museum (1982–87), during his pioneering research projects into unwritten aspects of the area's history.

The present staff of the museum, John Carter, Sue Grant and Nora Kavanagh have greatly assisted in compiling this book, as have two regular and long term volunteers, Norman Davie and Reg Wright. I am especially grateful to Barry Summers and Pam Aucott for letting me use material from their forthcoming books on (respectively) Harborough during the First World War and the early topographical photographs of the area.

Last, but by no means least, special thanks are due to Steve Thursfield and Catherine Broughton, of the Leicestershire Museums Photographic Service, for producing so many copy prints of the highest quality. As always, my wife Lynne has provided constant encouragement and help.

P. Abel • A. Atkins • S. Barker • J. Billing • D.M. Brotherton • F.H. Brown
E. Brown •M.C. Brown • B. Brown • W.F. Burbridge • A. Burton • Mr Capell
M. Carson • J. Carter • D. Chester • K. Coales • M. Coleman • A. Cornwell
J. Cousins • J.C. Davies • G. Davis • M. Eames • B. Elliott • E. Elliott
W. Falkner • M.J. Farey • P. Fox • C. Fraser • W.W. Frisby • F. Gerlach
S. Gibson • M. Goodwin • M. Greenwood • The Harboro' Rubber Company
A. Heggs • A. Hutchins • D. Jackson • F.C. Janes • B. Johnson • C.M. Law
D. Lewin • J. March • The Market Harborough Historical Society • H.G. Marlow
M. Monk • J. Morris • R. Murman • The National Railway Museum,York (p. 52)
A. & K. Noseworthy • M. O'Brien • G. Parke • R. Percival • G. Pickering
W. Rettig • R. Robinson • F.M. Rowe • J. Rowlatt • E. Savage • B. Sherry
A. Surridge • J. Swales • I. Symington • R. & W.H. Symington Ltd. • Symington &
Company • C. Tozer • F. Tuffs • Tungstone Batteries • H. Webb • A.G. Webb
N. Westley • E. White • Miss Wiggington • F. Willey • G. Williams
D. Wooldridge • R. Wright.